DATE DUE			
OC 17 '02			
NO 0 '0			

Printed
in USA

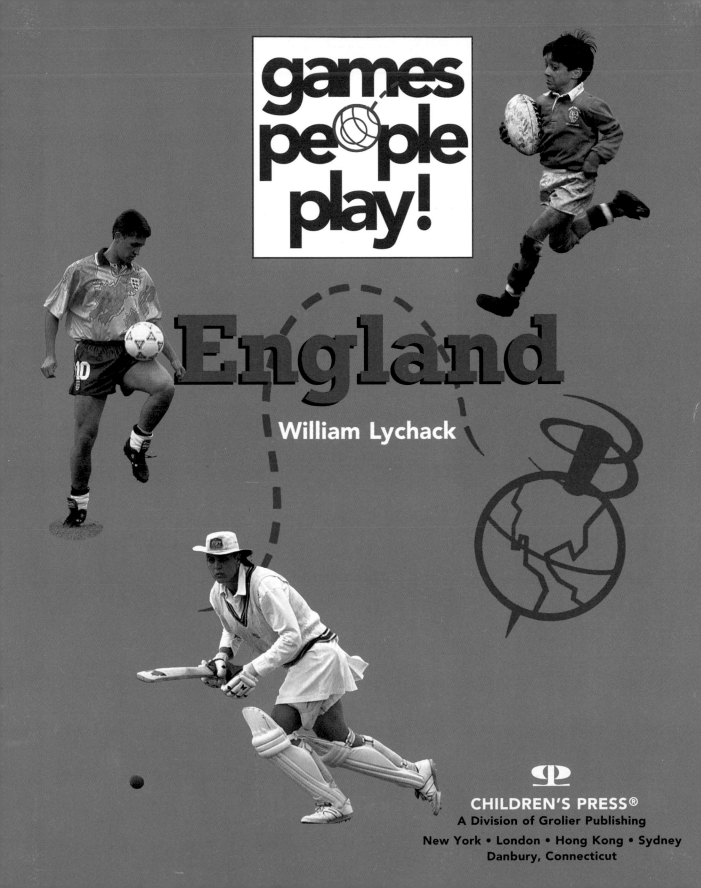

games people play!

England

William Lychack

CHILDREN'S PRESS®
A Division of Grolier Publishing
New York • London • Hong Kong • Sydney
Danbury, Connecticut

Editorial Staff

Project Editor: Mark Friedman

Photo Research: Feldman & Associates

Intern: Amy Vivio

Design Staff

Design and Electronic Composition: TJS Design

Maps: TJS Design

Cover Art and Icons: Susan Kwas

Activity Page Art: MacArt Design

Library of Congress Cataloging-in-Publication Data

Lychack, William

England / by William Lychack.

p. cm.—(Games people play)

Includes index.

Summary: Presents brief histories and descriptions of sports and recreations in England including cricket, soccer, rugby, horse sports, individual sports, pubs, and gardens.

ISBN 0-516-04436-2

1. Sports—England—History—Juvenile literature. 2. Recreation—England—History—Juvenile literature. 3. Ball games—England—History—Juvenile literature. 4. Horse sports—England—History—Juvenile literature. 5. Individual sports—England—History—Juvenile literature. [1. Sports—England. 2. Recreation—England.] I. Title. II. Series.

GV605.L93 1995   95-10109

796'.0942—dc20   CIP

                           AC

Table of **C**ontents

Introduction

England: The Glory of Traditions

Sports are more than just games to the people of England. Sports show the English people as they are — quirky, traditional, and fully civilized. Sportsmanship is a way of life to the English. From the Queen Mother to the Liverpool dock-worker, the way that games are played is much more important than who wins or loses.

Left: Big Ben, the famous clock tower connected to Britain's Houses of Parliament in London

Facing Page: The Henley Regatta is a gala, four-day festival of boating races on the Thames River at Henley-on-Thames. The races have been held since 1839.

England has enjoyed one of the most dramatic histories in the world. At its peak, it was said that the sun never set upon this great empire. At one time, the small island of Great Britain (of which England is a part) ruled more than a quarter of the entire world! It controlled many people and governments on six continents. To each of these distant colonies, the English brought their culture and

customs. Many English rulers regarded it as their duty to "civilize the world." This meant that they tried to force people in the British colonies to adopt England's customs, religion, and culture. Even now, after the English government no longer rules many of these colonies, the English way of life continues. For instance, people in the United States and Australia owe their language, their systems of law, and much of their culture to England.

A community's culture includes almost all the everyday things people do. Our culture is our civilization. It includes government, theater, music, literature, and sports. As England established political dominance around the world, it also affected the cultures of many countries. And just as they affected culture around the world, the English also changed the sports of the world. Boxing, tennis, soccer, rugby, and even table tennis all have origins in England. The English established the guidelines for safe and fair play in all of these games. They put gloves on boxers, for instance, to make the sport less brutal. They decided that deliberately kicking an opponent's shins ("hacking") was not to be allowed in soccer.

The many sports and games of England relate to different parts of its long history. For instance, the game of darts was originated by archers

culture

the things that define a community, including its government, art, and customs

The British are avid boaters — both for sport and relaxation. These boaters are on the Avon River.

many centuries ago. And foxhunting recalls England's history as an agricultural country with livestock to protect.

The traditions and rituals of games and sports have been passed down from generation to generation for countless years. Tradition keeps history alive, and most English people believe that as long as they keep firmly to their traditions, "there will always be an England."

ngland at a Glance

Land
England shares the island of Great Britain with Wales to the west and Scotland to the north. As an island, no part of England is more than one hundred miles from the sea. The English Channel separates Great Britain from mainland Europe. Located on the Thames River, London is one of the largest cities in the world. It is the thriving capital of England, as well as the focal point of the country's economy, arts, and growing tourism trade.

Government
England is part of the European nation called the United Kingdom of Great Britain and Northern Ireland. The British government system is called a "constitutional monarchy." This means that England maintains a throne — a king and/or queen. The duties of the crown are only ceremonial. The actual business of government is performed by Parliament, the prime minister, and the prime minister's cabinet.

People
Close to seven million people reside in London. More than 56 million people live in England as a whole. English people are commonly known as "Britons," "the British," or "the English." The official religious institution is the Anglican Church (the Church of England). Other major religions practiced are the Protestant religions, Roman Catholicism, and Judaism.

History
From 500 B.C. to A.D. 1066, England was invaded by a succession of conquerors: the Celts, Romans, Angles, Saxons, Danes, and Normans. These groups brought to England traditions of royal government, literature, and language that have survived to this day. Since the eleventh century, England has been ruled by a series of monarchs.

Because it is part of an island, England's economy has long relied on sea trade. With trade routes stretching throughout the world, England established many colonies in faraway lands. By the mid-1800s, England controlled colonies on six different continents. Some colonies (such as the United States and India) revolted and left the British Empire. Today, England has released most of its colonies, such as Hong Kong. But people in Scotland and Northern Ireland still seek freedom from English rule.

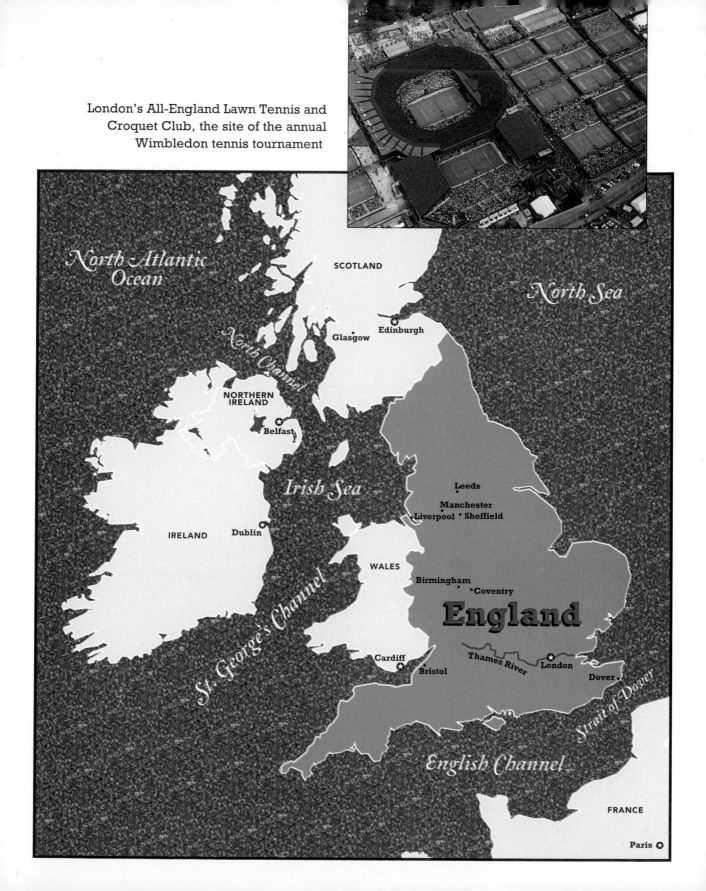

London's All-England Lawn Tennis and Croquet Club, the site of the annual Wimbledon tennis tournament

North Atlantic Ocean

SCOTLAND

North Sea

Glasgow

Edinburgh

North Channel

NORTHERN IRELAND

Belfast

Irish Sea

Leeds

Manchester

Liverpool • Sheffield

IRELAND

Dublin

WALES

Birmingham

Coventry

England

Cardiff

Thames River

London

Bristol

Dover

Strait of Dover

St. George's Channel

English Channel

FRANCE

Paris

Chapter One

Cricket: The National Pastime

Cricket has been called "the most English of games." It is a noble, unhurried sport of manners and graciousness. A cricketer will never argue with an umpire's decision. He will simply dust off his white flannel uniform and go along with the call.

With its long history of trying to civilize the world, it is only natural that England's most treasured sport is such a civil and orderly game. **Cricket** rules are not called rules —they are called "laws." This devotion to custom is what makes this game so English. What other country would schedule a lunch break and a tea time into its national pastime? Only England.

Cricket is one of England's oldest games. It dates back approximately eight hundred years. The game is thought to have been developed by shepherds. To pass the time as they tended their sheep, one shepherd would toss stones at a gate. Another shepherd would try to hit away the stones with his shepherd's crook (a type of walking stick). At that time, the shepherd's crook was called a "cric," hence the name of the game, "cricket."

A 1910 cricket club

Long ago in England, shepherds kept count of their sheep by cutting notches into their sticks. These notches were called "skors." That is how we get the word "score" today.

By 1700, cricket was being played under rules quite similar to those of today. As early as 1803, cricket had spread to Australia. Oddly enough, the first recorded international match was not played by England, but by the United States and Canada in 1844. Today, cricket is also played in such countries as Australia, India, New Zealand, Pakistan, and the West Indies.

Cricket is played in the summer, and some matches take place over four- or five-day stretches. Like American baseball, cricket is a bat-and-ball game that involves running from one base to another. In fact, there are many similarities between cricket and baseball because baseball developed out of cricket and another English game, rounders.

rounders

a bat-and-ball game from which cricket originated

A cricket bowler, whose job is similar to the pitcher in American baseball

Rules of the Game

Each team has 11 players. The fielding team has a bowler (similar to a baseball pitcher) who pitches a red leather ball at a stand of wickets.

Two wickets are placed 22 yards apart on each end of the bowling pitch. The pitch is the strip of grass between the two wickets.

Action begins as the bowler throws the ball toward the batsman, attempting to get the ball past the batsman and knock down the wicket. When this happens, the batsman is called "out," or "bowled out." The bowler may bounce the ball off the grass before it arrives at the batter. A bowler may not, however, bend his arm while throwing the ball.

Each team bats, or takes an innings, in turn. There are two batsmen on the field at all times, one at each wicket. The batsman hits the ball with a bat that is wide and flat at its end. A good batsman can stay at bat for hours and score many runs. Runs are scored when the batsman hits the ball and he and his partner run between the two wickets.

How Do I Play?

Cricket is a bat-and-ball sport similar to baseball. But cricket is a far more intricate and complex game. The difficulty of explaining how the game works is something of a national joke among the British. They say cricket is a game you must "feel" or "experience" more than understand.

One of the most entertaining parts of cricket is watching bowlers go through their windups to gain speed for the pitch. Once thrown, the ball can reach speeds of one hundred miles per hour.

Batsman

Bat

Ball

Wicket

On the Field

There are 11 players on the fielding team. Nine are positioned in the field to catch or stop the ball after it is batted. The other two players for the fielding team are the bowler and the wicket keeper. The wicket keeper (similar to the catcher in baseball) is the only fielder allowed to wear fielding gloves. Even with gloves, a wicket keeper's fingers are usually quite bruised. All the other fielders have to stop the hard ball with their bare hands and bodies. To make sure they stop the ball, fielders kneel down on one knee as the ball approaches.

The Cricket Field

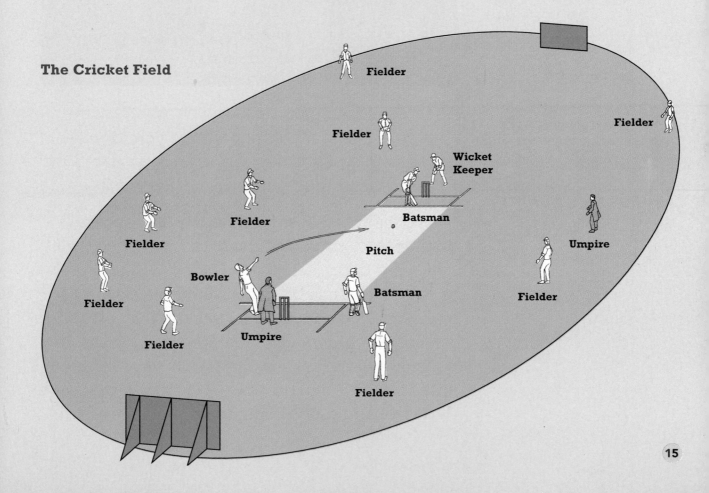

Fielder

Fielder

Fielder

Wicket
Keeper

Fielder

Fielder

Batsman

Umpire

Fielder

Bowler

Pitch

Batsman

Fielder

Fielder

Umpire

Fielder

Groundskeepers are known for taking meticulous care of the cricket grounds.

wicket

the five pieces of wood the bowler is trying to knock down; or the ground between the bowler and batsman

The best cricket grounds are cherished by the English. Care of a premier cricket field occupies at least six groundsmen. Strict laws govern how to roll and cut the grass on a cricket pitch.

Cricket spectators engage in lengthy debates about the condition of the pitch and how it will affect the day's match. The word "wicket" refers to the five pieces of wood which the bowler is trying to knock down. But "wicket" can also refer to the ground between the bowler and the batsman. A "batter's wicket" favors the batter and is usually dry and slow. A "sticky wicket" describes the ground after a rain. The grass is

Cricket in an English village

damp, and the ball's bounce is very unpredictable on such a field. To be in a sticky wicket means the batsman will have a difficult time hitting the ball. The bowler enjoys a good sticky wicket. That is, until he has to bat in his innings.

The traditional setting for a cricket match is an immaculate field surrounded by trees, with a church in the background chiming out the passing hours. Families bring large picnic hampers filled with food and drink and spend an entire day watching the match in the comfortable summer sunshine.

all-rounder

a cricket player who excels in more than one skill — one who can bat, bowl, and field well

William Gilbert Grace
The illustrious Grace Gates at Lord's memorialize the best cricketer who ever lived, W. G. Grace. He began his career in 1865 and dominated the game for the next 43 years. He scored 54,896 runs, an average of 39.55 per innings. He is called the "Babe Ruth" of cricket. And in addition to playing cricket, Grace was a medical doctor in Bristol.

Dr. W. G. Grace embodied the perfect gentleman cricketer. In 1891, he wrote a book entitled *Cricket*. In the book, he is modest about his achievements. He wrote that he wished good batsmen were born and not made. But he believed that "constant practice and sound coaching" brought him all of his success as a player.

With most traditional sports in England, there is usually a single event and location that is most important to the fans and the players. The most distinguished cricket ground is Lord's, founded by Thomas Lord in the 1800s. Lord's is located in Saint John's Wood, on the outskirts of London. Lord's serves as the headquarters of all cricket and is home to one of the oldest and most prestigious cricket clubs in the world, the Marylebone Cricket Club (MCC). This club has played the game at Lord's since 1814.

Every June, large crowds of spectators gather early in the morning outside Grace Gates at Lord's, hours before the gates open. These cricket fans are queuing up (the British term for "lining up") to see the highly anticipated Test Matches.

The Test Matches are international cricket's equivalent of baseball's World Series. Cricket fans look forward to the matches all year. A Test Match always takes place over five playing days of six hours each. A cricket match is called a "Test Match" if it is played between teams from a select group of first-class national teams. Cricket has grown and thrived in all of England's former colonies except one — the United States. The "test" countries include such former English colonies as Australia, India, and Pakistan. In addition to Lord's, other prestigious

Test Match grounds of England are The Oval in London, Trent Bridge in Nottingham, Old Trafford in Manchester, Edgbaston in Birmingham, and Headingly in Leeds.

These famous grounds are not the only places where cricket is played. Like American baseball or basketball, cricket fields can be found almost anywhere. Nearly every town or village supports a cricket team or club. It is England's most popular summer game. Women's cricket leagues are popular, as are those of colleges and public schools, the players no doubt dreaming of playing in one of the glorious Test Matches at Lord's.

The Oval in London, one of the most famous cricket grounds

Chapter Two

Soccer and Rugby

Almost two thousand years ago, Roman conquerors brought a game called "harpastum" to England with them. The Romans found, however, that the Irish and English peoples already played a similar game. The sport we today call "soccer" is a combination of these two games.

E ngland is the birthplace of **soccer**, and it is their most popular sport. Although cricket is considered a national symbol of England, many more people love and play soccer. In fact, soccer has spread to all continents, and it is now considered the most popular sport in the entire world. Some English believe that in a thousand years, soccer will be the one achievement for which England is most remembered. That is how proud they are of the sport they gave to the world!

In centuries past, the games that became soccer were extremely rough and very unruly. There were no rules about the number of players on a team, the size of the playing field, or how to move the ball. Huge mobs of people would fight and kick a ball toward goals that could be miles apart. Goals were sometimes at opposite ends of a village's main street. The population of an entire town would run up and down streets, moving in a loud, crazy riot. The earliest known reference to the game of soccer played in England is in a royal proclamation by King Edward II in 1314 — the king banned the game in London because of its violence and destructiveness.

A rowdy street soccer game during the Middle Ages

the soccer player who defends the goal

By the 1800s, English students at the universities and public schools played soccer games that were better organized, but were still fiercely fought. Every school or club across the country drew up its own set of rules. In 1843, fourteen of these schools and clubs came together at Cambridge University and agreed upon one set of rules. These rules remain the modern rules for today's soccer. Each team plays with eleven players. Goalkeepers are the only players who may hold the ball with their hands. Players in the field trap and handle the ball with any part of their bodies except their hands.

The league of fourteen schools and clubs that made the rules for soccer marked the founding of the Football Association of England. The Football Association (known as the "F. A.") is the world's oldest soccer organization.

It is believed the word "soccer" came from the letters "s-o-c" in the word "association." Another story is that the word came from the knee-high socks worn by most players. Perhaps, like the Irish and Roman ball games, the word "soccer" is a combination of both stories. In England, however, soccer is not commonly called "soccer." It is known as "football."

Women's soccer in England

F. A. Cup

England's national
championship soccer game

Soccer action at London's
famous Wembley Stadium

Association Football (soccer) is England's most popular sport, by far. Thousands of fans fill stadiums to watch the games. A cold afternoon with a cup of warm tea at a soccer match is thought to be a truly British experience.

In 1871, the F. A. Challenge Cup was introduced. To this day, the annual F. A. Cup remains England's national championship game. It is played in Wembley Stadium in London. Millions of soccer fans sit glued to televisions and radios in pubs all across the country as they follow the game.

English soccer fans remember the legendary soccer heroes of the past with the same reverence that Americans have for Babe Ruth, Ted Williams, or Joe DiMaggio. Sir Stanley Matthews and Bobby Charlton were two of the greatest soccer players in English history. Matthews played professional soccer for more than 30 years, and was the first soccer player to be knighted by a king in England. Charlton holds England's career record of 49 goals in international matches. His first was against Scotland in 1958, and his last was in 1970 against Columbia.

Today, England's Paul "Grazza" Gascoigne is one of the world's premier soccer talents. The English striker Gary Lineker is perhaps the country's best-loved soccer star. Lineker is known for his dedication to the game, as well as for his discipline and hard work.

British soccer star Gary Lineker

The followers of soccer teams in England are extraordinarily devoted. The term "fan" comes from the word "fanatic," and sometimes people at English soccer matches act like crazed fanatics. Soccer fans dress in team colors and paint their faces for the games. In the stadiums, fans yell elaborate calls back and forth, rival to rival. Many times, these rivalries get out of hand. This rowdiness can become especially violent when opposing teams represent different political or religious regions of the country. Fan violence has sometimes reached disastrous levels. Brutal fights among fans sometimes end in serious injury and even murder. The behavior of a few, violent fans, known as "hooligans," has led some observers to call this trend "the British Disease." The vast majority of Britons look upon this hooliganism as a terrible disgrace.

Liverpool fans cheer at an F. A. Cup final match.

England's national team celebrates after defeating West Germany for the 1966 World Cup.

The World Cup of 1966

Every four years, one of the world's great sports competitions takes place — the World Cup. In 1966, England hosted this grand festival of soccer. After progressing through the early rounds, England made it to the championship game. There, England defeated West Germany, 4-2 in overtime.

The 1966 English national team remains the most legendary sports team in English history. The squad was led by captain Bobby Moore. The star goalkeeper, Gordon Banks, played one of the best Cups in history. He allowed only six goals in the final six games, keeping England in close matches with several spectacular saves. Geoff Hurst turned in a hero's performance in the final game against the Germans. Hurst scored three goals (a hat trick) to help bring the Cup to England. No other player has ever scored as many goals in a final, not even the great Brazilian superstar Pelé. The manager of the team, Alf Ramsey, was knighted by the king of England.

Despite its glorious success in the 1966 World Cup, England could not successfully defend its Cup championship in 1970. Its fortunes in the World Cup tournament continued to decline, reaching a low point when it did not qualify for the tournament in 1994.

Players jostle for position as a pass is thrown in a rugby match.

Before the rules of soccer were set down clearly, the game was not much more than a free-for-all of kicking, hitting, and running. But there was one rule everyone obeyed: unless you were the goalkeeper, you did not hold the ball with your hands.

According to legend, **rugby** was born on an afternoon in 1823, when William Webb Ellis broke soccer's sacred no-hands rule. At a little past five o'clock at the Rugby School, Ellis was taking part in an interclass soccer match. The score was tied, and the game was supposed to have ended at five o'clock.

Bored by the slowness of the action, Ellis suddenly scooped up the ball in his hands, tucked it under his arm, and ran wildly toward the goal. His opponents chased him. His teammates chased him. People thought he had lost his mind! But Ellis made it across the goal, smiling and claiming victory. His teammates agreed. But the other team claimed he had cheated. So the teams played a rematch with the new rule that a player can touch the ball with his hands. The new game was called "rugby," named after the Rugby School where it was invented.

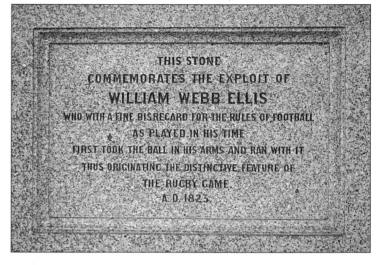

A memorial plaque at the Rugby School, birthplace of the game of rugby

Called "rugger" by those who play it today, rugby has evolved into a subtle, yet tough, game. Early rules allowed for matches that lasted more than five days and involved more than three hundred players! Today, the game is played with 13 or 15 players per side. But rugby is still a mix of mud, blood, and bruised bodies.

In many ways, the sport resembles American football because American football developed out of English rugby. The chief difference is that there is no forward pass in rugby. Teammates are allowed to carry, kick, and lateral the ball

scrum

players locking arms together, trying to gain possession of the ball

A rugby scrum

(throw it backwards) to one another. Meanwhile, opponents try to tackle the ballcarrier and to steal the ball away. The purpose of the game is to carry the ball across the goal line and "ground" it in the opponent's goal area. This is called a "try," and is worth four points.

One of the oddities of rugby takes place when teams face off for possession of the ball. The players all lock arms in a "scrum," or "scrummage." The tangle of arms and legs looks like a giant, muddy octopus. The players in the middle of this scrum are called "hookers," and they try to kick the ball with their heels out to their teammates behind them. The teammates attempt to pick up the ball and run with it. Just like William Webb Ellis, the team that can run across the goal line scores.

In 1895, an argument over paying money to players led to a split between rugby clubs in England. As a result, there are two leagues in England today—the professional (paid) Rugby League and the amateur (unpaid) Rugby Union.

Rugby also is played widely in Australia, New Zealand, and many other countries. In 1987, the first Rugby World Cup was played between national rugby teams from many countries. The second World Cup was played in 1995 in South Africa, a former colony of Great Britain.

Chapter Three

Equestrian Sports

Horses are expensive to buy and maintain. Aside from the initial cost of buying the horse, owners have to feed, stable, and equip the animal. Therefore, to use a horse for sports has always meant that a person must be very wealthy. So the equestrian sports (those involving horses) have been enjoyed mainly by England's powerful upper class.

A 1901 hunt meet

A foxhunt takes place on lush landscapes that seem to have jumped off the pages of a storybook. Before dawn, a person prepares the area for the hunt by sneaking around and blocking all the holes to the fox's den. Foxes are nocturnal — they hunt at night and sleep during the day. So when a fox returns to its den and finds the entrances blocked, it is forced to remain in the open during the hunt.

Early in the morning, the riders gather on their horses to start the hunt. The participants are called the "field," and the starting place is called the "meet." The mounted field can be as large as one hundred riders. The horses' manes are elegantly braided. And the riders are all dressed in proper hunting dress: red hunting coats, hats, and special pants called "jodhpurs."

The huntmaster is in charge of a foxhunt.

The hunt begins when the hounds are released to sniff for the scent of the fox. The hounds are followed by the huntmaster, the huntsman, and then the rest of the field. The huntmaster conducts the hunt and makes sure all aspects of it run smoothly.

The huntsman manages the hounds and makes sure they stay "on the scent" of the fox. Forty or fifty hounds usually make up a hunt pack. They are referred to as "foxhounds," never as "dogs." These hounds have been bred by the

Hounds in full cry

huntsman specifically for these chases. As the hounds find the scent of the fox, their barking becomes more intense — the hounds are "giving voice." A good huntsman can tell each individual hound by its own distinct bark and knows what each bark tone means.

As they ride along, everyone in the field awaits the yell of "Tally-Ho!" This is called out by the first member of the field who sees the fox. When the fox finally is cornered, the hounds usually kill it. The hounds will eat everything except the fox's brush (tail), mask (head), and pads (paws). These will be awarded as trophies to members of the field, usually to the first rider to reach the site of the kill.

The sport of foxhunting dates back to the early 1400s. The foxes were killed because they destroyed farmers' livestock. Rewards were given to people who got rid of the foxes.

Foxhunting became popular as a sport in the mid-1700s. People who love foxhunting claim that the fox actually enjoys the challenge of outsmarting the hounds and the field. In modern times, however, the morality of the foxhunt has been called into question. Many people think it is wrong to hunt and kill an animal for sport. English animal-rights groups now attempt to stop the hunts. Members of these groups sneak into the area of the hunt and trick the hounds with false whistles and misleading scents.

In recent years, some hunt clubs have given up pursuing a live fox. They carry out their hunts with artificial scents. These hunts are called "draghunts" because someone will drag the odor of a fox through the thickets and hedges, tricking the hounds into thinking that they are chasing a fox. This more humane trend in foxhunting shows that the real sport is not the killing of the fox. The thrill of the hunt is the chase, the well-trained hounds, the horsemanship, and the beauty of the English countryside.

British soldiers brought **polo** home from India in 1871, and the game has been a favorite for horsemen ever since. Many riders believe that polo is the proving ground of great horse riding skills. Polo also is an exciting game to watch, and it is easy to understand. Four players ride for each team and try to drive a wooden ball into their opponent's goal with long-handled mallets. The polo field is the largest of any sport. Because they must run such great distances, the sport is very hard on the polo horses, called "ponies." The rules of the game allow for the horses to be rested after each seven-and-a-half-minute period. A game lasts for eight of these periods, called "chukkers."

chukkers

seven-and-a-half-minute periods in a game of polo

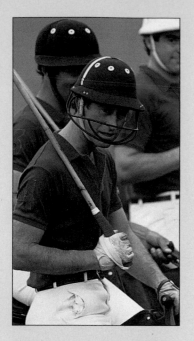

For many years, **Prince Charles** has been a well-known and highly competent polo player. The prince plays with a handicap of four, which places him among the best polo players in the world. As in golf, a player's handicap is the number of points taken off his score to even the competition among players of differing abilities.

As the first son of the queen (herself a noted authority on horses), Prince Charles is heir apparent to the throne. This means that when his mother dies, Charles will likely ascend to the throne and become the next king of England.

English polo is played among private clubs that are very exclusive and expensive to join. Still, many people flock to the games. For the most part, the clubs are less formal than we might think. It is important for spectators to wear comfortable shoes, particularly if taking part in the odd custom of "stamping in the divots." At half-time and between games, everyone flocks onto the polo ground and stamps their feet. They are replacing "divots," which are clumps of grass and mud that have been kicked up by the horses' hooves.

Another equestrian sport is dressage — a competition that displays the beautiful physique of the horse, as well as its training.

In dressage, horses display various paces, halts, and changes of direction. They are judged on their precision.

The earliest horse races in England date back to A.D. 200. These races were held by the Romans when they occupied England. The Romans introduced the speedy Arabian horses to England.

The finish of the Epsom Derby in 1935

One of the first sweepstakes races was organized in 1780 by the twelfth Earl of Derby at his estate in Epsom, England. The race has been held annually ever since. The Earl of Derby's race was so popular that the word "derby" is now used to describe any important horse race (such as the most important U.S. horse race, the Kentucky Derby). The legendary jockey named Lester Piggott has won the Epsom Derby more times than anyone — an incredible total of nine championships.

Action at the Royal Ascot (below). At this historic racetrack, fans traditionally watch the Gold Cup race in formal dress (right).

Another famous English horse race is the Gold Cup, held at the Royal Ascot racing grounds. Races at the Ascot are noted for the beautiful and sometimes strange hats worn by the spectators. (The Earl of Derby might have enjoyed this race, too, having had a hat [the bowler] named after him, also!)

These horse races are all "flat" races, meaning that they are run on a flat field or track. A popular English variation on flat horse racing is the **steeplechase**, in which the racecourse takes the horses over a series of jumps. Steeplechases are generally associated with foxhunting clubs in England. In one of these races, jockeys lead their horses (called "mounts") through three miles of fences, ditches, and water jumps. Because many of these races are still set in the country, most of the spectators are usually local farmers. This type of race came to be known as a "steeplechase" because the riders always kept in sight of the local church steeple.

A horse takes a jump during a steeplechase race.

The most prized race among steeplechase riders is the Grand National. The first Grand National Handicap Steeplechase was run in 1839 just outside of Liverpool, England. One of the most famous horses in British equestrian history was named Red Rum. He is the only horse to win the Grand National three times — in 1973, 1974, and 1977 (and he came in second in 1975 and 1976)!

jockey
person who rides
a horse in a horse race

Chapter Four

Individual Sports

"Pluck" is a quality valued by the English.

It means fighting hard and fair, and fighting

to the very end, win or lose. It is a compliment

in England to call someone "plucky."

Many English people love tough individual games and contests because they test a person's pluck. To "pluck up your heart" is an old boxing phrase. To "pluck up" one's heart is to pick oneself up in a dire, tight situation.

Boxing is an ancient sport that demands pluck. Boxing has roots as far back as ancient Rome. It emerged in the 1600s as a popular British sport in such port cities as Liverpool and Bristol. The people there worked long, hard hours in factories or on the docks. Fabulous stories still are told of the brutally strong dockworkers who would box for a few shillings. Bloody men fought each other savagely with their bare hands. A round lasted until one fighter fell down or was knocked down. The downed fighter had 30 seconds to "get back to scratch" (to get up on his feet). If he failed to do this, he lost the match. To the delight of large crowds (most of whom had wagered money on the fight), bouts often lasted 50 or more rounds! It was often difficult to know who was the winner of these brutal fights. In the end, both fighters were bloody, bruised, and staggering.

Opposite Page:
British runner Sally Gunnell, gold medalist in the 400-meter hurdles in the 1992 Summer Olympics

RULES

TO BE OBSERVED IN ALL BATTLES ON THE STAGE

I. That a square of a yard be chalked in the middle of the Stage; and on every fresh set-to after a fall, or being parted from the rails, each Second is to bring his Man to the side of the square, and place him opposite to the other, and till they are fairly set-to at the Lines, it shall not be lawful for one to strike at the other.

II. That, in order to prevent any Disputes, the time a Man lies after a fall, if the Second does not bring his Man to the side of the square, within the space of half a minute, he shall be deemed a beaten Man.

III. That in every main Battle, no person whatever shall be upon the Stage, except the Principals and their Seconds; the same rule to be observed in bye-battles, except that in the latter, Mr. Broughton is allowed to be upon the Stage to keep decorum, and to assist Gentlemen in getting to their places, provided always he does not interfere in the Battle; and whoever pretends to infringe these Rules to be turned immediately out of the house. Every body is to quit the Stage as soon as the Champions are stripped, before the set-to.

IV. That no Champion be deemed beaten, unless he fails coming up to the line in the limited time, or that his own Second declares him beaten. No Second is to be allowed to ask his man's Adversary any questions, or advise him to give out.

V. That in bye-battles, the winning man to have two-thirds of the Money given, which shall be publicly divided upon the Stage, notwithstanding any private agreements to the contrary.

VI. That to prevent Disputes, in every main Battle the Principals shall, on coming on the Stage, choose from among the gentlemen present two Umpires, who shall absolutely decide all Disputes that may arise about the Battle; and if the two Umpires cannot agree, the said Umpires to choose a third, who is to determine it.

VII. That no person is to hit his Adversary when he is down, or seize him by the ham, the breeches, or any part below the waist: a man on his knees to be reckoned down.

As agreed by several Gentlemen at Broughton's Amphitheatre, Tottenham Court Road, August 16, 1743.

A reproduction of Jack Broughton's first rules for boxing

Jack Broughton was a 1700s boxing champ who set down the first code of rules for the boxing ring. One of his innovations was "mufflers" to be worn on the hands. These eventually led to today's boxing gloves. Broughton's formal boxing rules included: no biting, no kicking, no eye-gouging, no head-butting, and no low blows (below the belt). His code of ethics suggests just how savage boxing once was.

Broughton's code was a big step toward taming boxing into a science and an art. New rules categorized fighters by weight so that a fighter would not significantly outsize his opponent. Fighters could no longer hit a man when he was down. And not every bout ended in a knockout — fighters scored points, and the referee could stop the fight if one fighter was being beaten badly.

The new style of boxing marked a change in the definition of an English gentleman. Rather than using swords and pistols to settle disputes, men in England began to tie on gloves and enter boxing rings. A question of honor was no longer a life-or-death matter for the Englishman. Boxing became a way of settling such matters.

Tennis has come a long way from its beginnings in the 1800s. Gone are the days when men had to wear long white flannels, and women wore bloomers and lovely straw hats. Today's game is fast, aggressive, and highly competitive. Both men's and women's tennis are followed avidly in England.

The sport of tennis began in France, but Major Walter C. Wingfield of England patented the rules and equipment of the modern game in 1874. Soon, tennis replaced croquet as one of England's favorite outdoor sports. In 1877, the All-England Croquet Club changed its name to the All-England Lawn Tennis and Croquet Club. This club is the host for Wimbledon, the oldest and most prestigious tennis tournament in the world.

In the early 1900s, women in England played tennis wearing long, heavy dresses.

English Versatility
Charlotte Dod was certainly the most versatile athlete in Britain. Historians say she was one of the greatest athletes in modern history.

Lottie, as she was called, won the Wimbledon singles tennis title five times between 1887 and 1893. At 15 years old, she was the youngest person ever to win the tournament.

But Lottie's athletic skills were not limited to tennis. She also won the British Ladies Golf Championship in 1904 and an Olympic silver medal for archery in 1908, and she represented England in hockey at the Olympics in 1899. She also excelled at figure skating!

The All-England Club is the keeper of many of tennis's earliest traditions. It still maintains such rules as a strict dress code. To this day, all players must wear white in order to play at Wimbledon. Wimbledon tennis matches are played on grass, like early lawn tennis. (Almost all other major tournaments in the world are played on clay or on indoor courts.)

English tennis legend Bill Tilden, who won six consecutive Wimbledon men's titles (1920–25)

The annual Wimbledon tournament lasts for two weeks in the middle of summer. Even though it is more than a century old, Wimbledon retains its prominence as the high point of the international tennis season. As the Australian player Rod Laver said after winning the Wimbledon trophy: "What is there left to prove?" The last English citizen to win at Wimbledon was Virginia Wade, in 1977. It took 15 years of striving for her to win the world's most sought-after tennis award.

Wimbledon is one of the four international tournaments that make up the "Grand Slam" of tennis; the others are the Australian Open, the French Open, and the U.S. Open. Of the four, Wimbledon is the most prestigious. Modern tennis heroes who have dominated at Wimbledon include Pete Sampras (left) and Martina Navratilova (right, holding the Wimbledon women's trophy).

Roger Bannister makes history in 1954 by breaking the four-minute mile.

When Roger Bannister entered Oxford University to study medicine, he was told, "A man without a sport is like a ship without a sail." Under pressure to choose a sport, Bannister chose **running**. Little could he have known that he would run his way into the hearts of every English citizen and become a national and international hero.

Like climbing Mount Everest or going to the moon, people long had thought that running a mile in four minutes or less was impossible. Not as long as the marathon nor as short as a dash, the mile race is a great test of both speed and stamina. On May 6, 1954, Roger Bannister became the first man to run a mile in less than four minutes. His achievement still is remembered as one of the greatest moments in English sport. Bannister was knighted by Queen Elizabeth in 1975.

In recent years, England has maintained its high stature in the world of running. Daley Thompson won Olympic gold medals in 1980 and 1984 for the decathlon. This Olympic event combines ten different track-and-field events involving running, jumping, and throwing. Decathlon champions are considered among the greatest athletes in the world, a status Daley Thompson enjoyed for many years. In 1992, Linford Christie won the Olympic gold medal in the 100-meter dash, a feat that immediately crowned him as the fastest man alive.

decathlon

Olympic competition combining ten track-and-field events

Linford Christie (center) claims the gold medal in the 100-meter dash at the 1992 Olympics.

Matthew Webb swimming the English Channel in 1875

Chunnel

tunnel that runs under the English Channel and connects England to France; began operating in 1994

Beneath the waters of the English Channel, the new Channel Tunnel (called "Chunnel") connects England to France. Between Dover, England, and the coast of France lies twenty-one miles of water. This channel has proved a worthy moat and has protected England against invasion for the last nine hundred years. The voyage from shore to shore has forever been a challenge to foreign conquerors, as well as to the brave and daring Channel swimmers.

A twenty-one-mile **swim** might not seem like a big challenge, but the English Channel is a tough 21 miles. These are dangerous, murky waters. The Channel's currents are strong and tricky. The first person officially to complete the swim was Matthew Webb in 1875. He completed the task in 21 hours and 45 minutes. The fastest swim was performed by Penny Dean on July 29, 1978. She swam the Channel in just 7 hours and 45 minutes.

The youngest swimmer to conquer the Channel was Marcus Hooper of Great Britain. He swam from Dover to Sangette, France, in 1979, when he was just 12 years old. The youngest girl was Samantha Claire Druce, also of Great Britain. She was also 12 (but a few days older than Marcus Hooper) when she swam the Channel in 1983.

Some daredevil swimmers are not satisfied to cross the channel just once. Michael Read has made the swim 31 times. And there are swimmers who complete the channel swim more than one time in succession. The first triple-crossing of the channel (completing three back-to-back crossings) was by Jon Erickson in 1981. He swam from England to France three consecutive times in a total of 31 hours, 27 minutes.

Covered in protective grease, Gertrude Ederle emerges from the water after becoming the first woman to swim the Channel, in 1926.

51

Chapter Five

A Long History of Fun and Games

There are virtually no aspects of British culture that do not carry some hint of the island's rich history. In fact, many games and activities that English children and adults play can be traced directly to some episode from England's long, storied history.

The well-known song and game "London Bridge is Falling Down" dates back to the eleventh-century invasion of London by Norway's King Olaf and his soldiers. In the fighting, King Olaf ordered the destruction of the great London Bridge, which spanned the Thames River.

To play "London Bridge," two players (the bridge-keepers) clasp hands and hold them high to make a tunnel for the rest of the players to pass under. While the players walk under the "bridge," they sing the well-known song. The first verse is:

London Bridge is falling down,
Falling down, falling down.
London Bridge is falling down,
My fair lady.

Upon "lady" (the final word of each verse), the bridge-keepers lower their hands, and the player they trap is put in "prison" and eliminated from the game.

Above: Old London Bridge, which was rebuilt after its destruction

Facing Page: Lawn bowling, a favorite British sport

Children around the world love to play the game **"Ring Around the Rosy."** This is another child's song and game that tells a story, this time of a terrible event from Britain's past. The simple game consists of children dancing in a circle while holding hands. The first verse of the song goes:

Ring around the rosy,
A pocket full of posies
Ashes, ashes,
We all fall down!

The song chanted during this game refers to the Great Plague that struck London in 1664 and caused widespread death. Most players do not know it, but these words actually refer to the gruesome effects of the deadly plague. For instance, "Ring around the rosy" refers to the plague symptom of lesions or sores on the skin, which have red circles. And because there were so many funerals during the plague years, the words "ashes, ashes" refer to the phrase from funeral services, "Ashes to ashes, dust to dust." After the word "down," all the players drop to a sitting position while still holding hands. They make believe they are dead.

According to one legend, **hopscotch** developed in England when the country was occupied centuries ago by Roman conquerors. It is a game similar to one played by soldiers from Rome. Many of the first hopscotch courts were more than one hundred feet in length. These courts imitated the long, four-hundred-mile journey along the Great North Road, which ran from London to Scotland. This is how the game got the name "hopscotch"— meaning hopping to Scotland, the home of the Scotch people. Often, Roman players would hop through the courses carrying heavy loads (or other soldiers) on their backs to test their strength.

Sidewalks and schoolyards all over England are decorated with colorful, chalk-drawn boxes where children play hopscotch.

English children also love to play the hide-and-seek game, **fox and hounds**. In this game, one player (the fox) runs and hides from the rest of the players (the hounds). Another game played at many children's parties is called **ha, ha, ha**. Two or more players sit in a circle. One player starts by saying, "Ha." The next says, "Ha, ha." Each player must add a "Ha" to the string, but everyone must say the funny words quite seriously. If someone laughs or forgets how many "Ha's" to say, he or she is eliminated from the game. The most serious player — the one who does not laugh and keeps count — wins the game.

Draughts is the English version of checkers, and is a longtime favorite of English children. The game was born long ago when someone decided to use backgammon pieces on a chessboard.

A giant, outdoor chess-board on an English city square. Chess has been popular in England for more than six centuries.

Nothing is as important to a British adult as his or her local pub. Short for "public house," pubs are cozy places where people from all walks of life gather over pints of ale, fish and chips, meat-and-kidney pie, and good talk and games. Several card games are popular in English pubs.

Whist first appeared in England in 1529 and was the world's favorite card game through the nineteenth century. It is a four-person game somewhat similar to bridge, a card game popular around the world today. Bridge developed out of whist about a century ago. **Cribbage** was invented by the English dramatist Sir John Suckling in the 1600s. It is a card game for two, three, or four people in which players' scores are kept with wooden pegs on a pegboard.

Playing snooker in a pub

Another popular pub game is **snooker**. This is a form of billiards using only 15 red balls and six of other colors. It was invented in 1875 by Sir Neville Francis Fitzgerald, an Englishman living in the British colony of India.

By far, the most popular English pub game is **darts**. Darts developed out of archery. Centuries ago, archers used bows and arrows for hunting. But they also carried smaller arrows for close-range fighting. Archers practiced by throwing these long darts into

Pub-goers play darts, the most popular pub game in England.

trees. Since they wanted to keep practicing during cold winters, the archers brought sawed-off sections of trees inside. These were the first dartboards.

Today, there are an estimated seven million dart players in the British Isles. There is a professional dart league in Great Britain. England's Eric Bristow has captured virtually every existing darts championship. He has won the World Masters Championship five times, the World Professional Championship five times, and the World Cup Singles crown four times!

A British family enjoys one of the many stunning vistas in the English countryside.

British people love the outdoors. Many British families enjoy going off into the country for hiking, or trekking, expeditions across the magnificent English landscape. Rowing is a vigorous sport that remains popular at many British universities. The most famous rowing event is the Henley Royal Regatta, which has taken place at Henley-on-Thames in Oxfordshire since 1839. The race is more than a mile long and attracts huge crowds. In addition to being the premier regatta in the world, it is one of the biggest social occasions on the English calendar.

British families love spending time in their gardens, where they play many sports and games. **Lawn bowling**, or "bowls," can be traced back to ancient Egypt, Greece, and Rome, and has been played in England for some nine centuries. The game involves rolling balls across a closely cut lawn called a "green."

The bowling green is much like a golf green. The object is to hit a small, white target ball with the larger, heavier black balls. Lawn bowling is similar to **croquet**, an ancient French game that involves hitting balls through wickets with a wooden mallet.

Also similar to croquet, but on a much larger scale, is **golf**. This is yet another sport with roots in many ancient civilizations, but the game as we know it began in Scotland in the 1700s.

On the putting green during the British Open

Naturally, the game then spread throughout the British colonies and, therefore, around the world. Today, one of the world's most prestigious golf tournaments is the British Open, which began in 1860, and is played every year at the St. Andrews course in Scotland.

lossary

colony
a community and a piece of land that is controlled and owned by a foreign government; before the Revolutionary War, the American colonies were controlled by England

constitutional monarchy
a system of government (such as in England) in which there is a monarch (king or queen) who is a figurehead; the actual work of the government is performed by elected officials, such as the prime minister and the Parliament

croquet
a backyard game played with wooden mallets and balls

divot
a chunk of soil and grass dug up by a horse's hoof (or, in golf, by a golf club that hits the ground)

dressage
an equestrian sport in which a horse's physique and abilities are judged in competition

equestrian
sports that involve riding horses

fan
a spectator devoted to a sports team; short for "fanatic"

field
foxhunting term referring to the riders and horses participating in a hunt

football
the European term for soccer (as opposed to American football)

ale
a dark, bitter beer, usually served at room temperature

batsman
the cricket player who attempts to hit the ball with a bat after it has been thrown by the bowler

bowler
the cricket player who throws the ball at the batsman (similar to the pitcher in baseball)

civility
courtesy or politeness; to "civilize" is to bring law and order to an unruly community

hat trick
three goals by one player in a single game; derived from cricket, in which bowlers were once given a cap (or hat) if they struck out three consecutive batsmen

hooligan
a rough, violent person who causes trouble and does not care about others' safety

hound
the type of dog used to chase the scent of the fox in a foxhunt

huntsman
the person who trains and controls the hounds for a foxhunt

mallet
long-handled sticks with heads; used to hit the ball in polo and croquet

match
the British term for a "game"

pitch
narrow strip of short grass in center of cricket field

pluck
courage in the face of a difficult situation; determination

ponies
the term used to describe horses used in a polo match

ring
the square clearing in the center of a crowd in which boxers fight

rugger
another name for rugby

scrum
a rugby term referring to the pileup of players fighting for control of the ball

test match
a cricket game involving teams from different countries

wicket
a small gate; refers to the stakes that a cricket bowler tries to hit with the ball; also refers to the condition of the cricket field

Index

(**Boldface** page numbers indicate illustrations.)

Photo Credits

About the Author

William Lychack works in Minneapolis, Minnesota, as a writer and editor. He was educated at Connecticut College and the University of Michigan. He has taught at the University of Michigan, Middlebury College, and the University of Minnesota, and he has been an editor at *New England Review*. His fiction has appeared in many quarterly magazines, including *Ascent*, *Seattle Review*, *Witness*, *Quarterly West*, and others. He has lived, for short periods of time, in London.